THE HERITAGE COLLECTION

Kandake Amanirenas

Defender of Kush

Letitia deGraft Okyere

Illustrated by Nouman Zafar

Kandake Amanirenas: Defender of Kush

Copyright © 2023 by Letitia deGraft Okyere

Illustrator: Nouman Zafar

Layout designer: Nassim Sarkar

Library of Congress Control Number: 2023901311

All rights reserved.

No part of this publication may be reproduced, stored in a retrieval system, a database, and/or published in any form or by any means, electronic, mechanical, photocopying, recording or otherwise, without the prior written permission of the publisher.

ISBN 978-1-956776-14-0 hardcover
ISBN 978-1-956776-15-7 ebook

Published by Lion's Historian Press
https://www.lionshistorian.net/

For

Elinam and Edem

A Brief Introduction

Today, we are in the year 2023 or AD 2023. AD is used to describe a period on the calendar. It is short for anno Domini, meaning in the year of our Lord, referring to the years after the birth of Jesus Christ. Before AD was the period known as BC, or before Christ. The last year of the BC period was 1 BC, and that was followed by the year AD 1, the first year of the AD period. Kandake Amanirenas lived over two thousand years ago, during the last century or hundred years of the BC period.

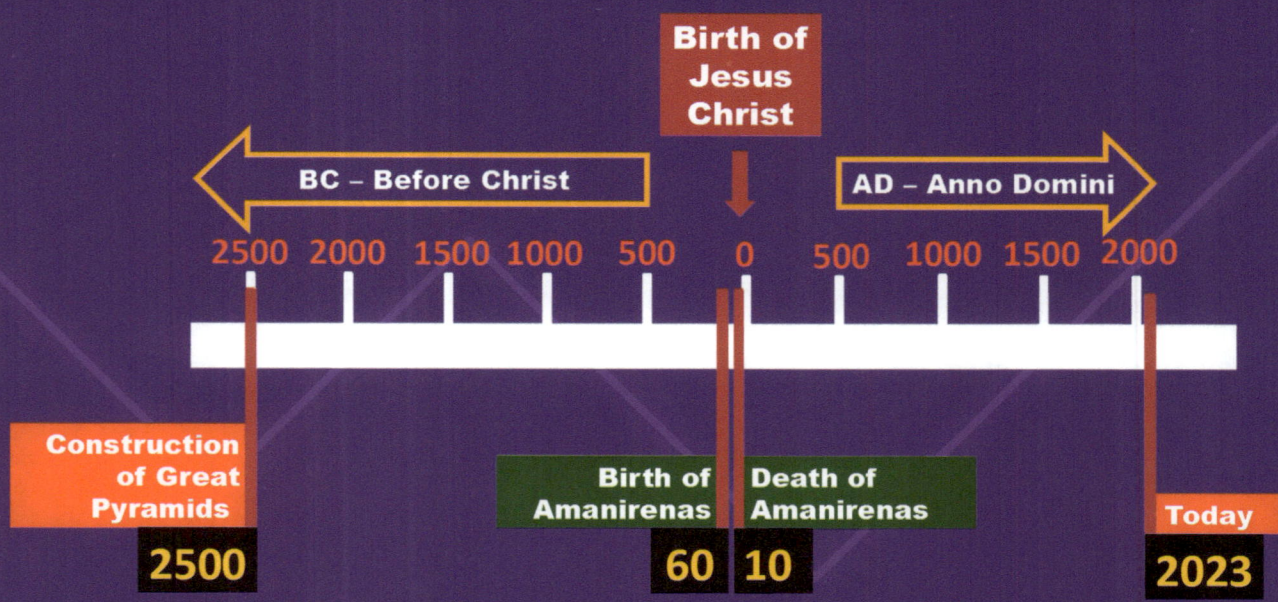

Contents

Chapter 1: A Queen of Meroë 1

Chapter 2: The Kingdom of Kush at Meroë 3

Chapter 3: Warrior Training 5

Chapter 4: Roman Expansion Plans 7

Chapter 5: Rumors of an Attack on Kush 9

Chapter 6: Battle with the Romans 11

Chapter 7: Romans Retake Syene and Philae 13

Chapter 8: The Kushite Return 15

Chapter 9: Kushite Emissaries to Rome 17

Chapter 10: The Legacy of Amanirenas 19

Glossary 21

Quiz 23

References 24

Fun Fact About the Nile River 25

Other Books in the Heritage Collection 26

Chapter - 1

A Queen of Meroë

Amanirenas was a queen of Meroë, and her full title was *Amnirense qore li Amanirenas* (ruler and Kandake). Amanirenas held the title qore because she ruled as a queen. She is believed to have been a joint monarch with her husband, known as Teritegas, and after his death, she ruled the kingdom alone. Amanirenas was a Kandake or *royal woman* because her son, Prince Akinidad, was heir to the throne.

Historians write that Amanirenas was born around 60 BC in the Kingdom of Kush. Kush was a state in ancient Nubia and referred to an area around the Nile River, covering parts of modern-day southern Egypt and northern Sudan in Africa. Amanirenas became the sole monarch around 40 BC, one of several queens who reigned in Kush.

Chapter - 2

The Kingdom of Kush at Meroë

Kandake Amanirenas was the second woman to rule during the time when the Kingdom of Kush was at Meroë. Kush had two old capital cities, Kerma and Napata, higher up the Nile River. At the time of Amanirenas' reign, when the capital was at Meroë, the kingdom was at its most advanced stage. It was a leading city in the ancient world. They had a water supply system and built many pyramids.

The people of Kush, known as Kushites, once used writing like Egyptian hieroglyphics or picture words. During the Meroë period, Kushites developed writing that used a combination of hieroglyphics and letters. As a result, the rulers of Meroë, like Kandake Amanirenas, left writings on stones known as *stelae*. As it is a complex form of writing, modern historians are unable to understand it.

However, a Greek writer who lived about the same time as Kandake Amanirenas recorded that she was a powerful leader. Kandake Amanirenas was a fierce fighter who protected her kingdom.

Chapter - 3

Warrior Training

In the Kingdom of Kush, both boys and girls learned to use the bow and arrow from an early age. Egyptians who lived to the north of Kush referred to the Nubian region as the *Land of the Bow*. Amanirenas was determined to be skillful with the bow and arrow and took many lessons. Before long, she was winning contests against other members of the royal household. Later, legends grew about Amanirenas' ability to attack enemies with a bow and arrow, riding an elephant.

Amanirenas would need to depend on her warrior skills many times, particularly after her husband Teritegas died, making her ruler over Kush. As Meroë was lower down the Nile River than the other previous Kush capital cities, it had rich forests and fertile land that produced abundant grain and supported nomads who grazed their flock. Weavers grew flax and cotton, making fabric on looms. Hunters' prized leopard skins and elephant tusks were traded along the Nile River toward Egypt. In addition, the land had a flourishing iron industry and was rich with copper, ivory, and gold. Thus, Meroë attracted traders and visitors from neighboring regions who wanted to conquer Nubia, including Kush.

Chapter - 4

Roman Expansion Plans

Amanirenas watched with concern as the Roman soldier, Octavian, who would become known as Roman Emperor Caesar Augustus, fought with his rival Marc Anthony. The dispute spread to Egypt because of Marc Anthony's friendship with the Egyptian Queen Cleopatra. In 31 BC, Octavian defeated Marc Anthony and Cleopatra in battle, and he took control of Egypt, making it a Roman province. Egypt was north of Kush, and Kandake Amanirenas sensed that Octavian, now Roman Emperor Caesar Augustus, would seek to extend his empire to Nubia, putting Kush at risk.

Kandake Amanirenas believed that Kushite soldiers must prepare for battle against a likely Roman attack. The region was important to the Romans because of access to trade and grain. Amanirenas called a meeting of her generals and instructed them to begin training.

Chapter - 5

Rumors of an Attack on Kush

Soon, Kandake Amanirenas heard rumors of a possible Roman attack on Kush. The Romans had made plans to conquer additional land and tried to place a tax on Kushite neighbors living in Nubia. Kandake Amanirenas also grew unhappy with the Romans, who had set up a frontier at a settlement called Syene, modern-day Aswan. Syene was a border town in southern Egypt, facing Nubia. This was seen as a threat by Kandake Amanirenas.

The Kushites were worried because the Romans had a larger empire with more soldiers and advanced battle tactics. Kandake Amanirenas reassured her people that she had a plan to withstand a Roman attack. Amanirenas decided to strike first. As the Romans had a stronger army, the benefit of a surprise attack would help Kush secure a victory. She asked her generals to begin a march to the region north of Kush, at the border of Egypt and Nubia.

Chapter - 6

Battle with the Romans

Kandake Amanirenas and her son, Prince Akinidad, led an army of thirty thousand warriors up to Egypt. At the time, Emperor Caesar Augustus had appointed Aelius Gallus governor of Egypt. When Aelius Gallus went on a military campaign to Arabia in 24 BC, a part of Roman plans to control large areas, Kandake Amanirenas realized it was the best time to strike. She knew that Gallus was at a disadvantage because there were rumors that his Arabian war was a failure.

The Kushite warriors, led by Kandake Amanirenas and her son Prince Akinidad, fought with the Romans at Syene and Philae. Kandake Amanirenas and her warriors defeated the Romans. She captured three Roman cities, many slaves, and Roman statues in Egypt, including some of Caesar Augustus. She destroyed a bronze statue of Emperor Caesar Augustus, cutting off its head. In a final show of victory over the Romans, she buried the bronze head underneath the entrance to a public building in Meroë. Kushites had humbled Augustus because they *walked over his head* every time they went into the building.

Chapter - 7

Romans Retake Syene and Philae

Kandake Amanirenas got ready for a new battle when she heard that Caesar Augustus had removed Aelius Gallus from his position as governor of Egypt and replaced him with Gaius Petronius, a military commander. Augustus was disappointed that Aelius Gallus failed to defeat the Kushites.

The Kushites found themselves faced with ten thousand Roman soldiers around 22 BC. Kandake Amanirenas led Kushite forces alone, as Prince Akinidad had died in battle. The Roman soldiers drove the Kushites out of Syene and traveled deep into Kush. They destroyed the old Kushite capital city called Napata and took about one thousand slaves.

The fighting between Amanirenas and the Kushites against the Romans was fierce. A Roman soldier close to Kandake Amanirenas flicked his sword and destroyed an eye. The Romans believed the destruction of Napata and Amanirenas' injury meant that the Kushites would never revolt against them. They went up north and set up a new boundary at Primis in Nubia. The Romans failed to recognize Kandake Amanirenas' determination to ensure her kingdom was not enslaved. The Roman destruction in Kush encouraged her to keep fighting. She refused to accept defeat.

Chapter - 8

The Kushite Return

After three years, when Kandake Amanirenas had healed from her injuries, she decided to capture the land taken by the Romans and assembled her warriors. Kandake Amanirenas led the march to recapture Primis and push the Romans out of Nubia.

Kandake Amanirenas swiftly dealt with Roman attacks and caused them many losses. She became known as the one-eyed Kushite queen, and stories of her war elephants and pet lions grew. The difficult battle for Primis left both sides wondering how long the conflict would last. The Romans were exhausted by the Kushite resilience, and Kandake Amanirenas was concerned about the increasing number of deaths among her soldiers. It was time for a new strategy, she thought.

Chapter - 9

Kushite Emissaries to Rome

Kandake Amanirenas sent emissaries to Caesar Augustus to negotiate a peace treaty. Amanirenas traded on the Roman losses, arguing that the Kushites were unlikely to admit defeat. Though the Romans had a superior army and more advanced weapons, there were several factors helping the Kushites. First, due to the distance to Nubia, the Romans had problems getting supplies to the soldiers. Second, the Kushite warriors were more familiar with the area.

Thus, after several years of battle, around 21 BC, Kandake Amanirenas signed a peace treaty with Rome. The Kushites did not have to pay taxes to Rome, and neither did Kush become a source of food supply for the Romans. Instead, Amanirenas established a trade system with the Romans and returned all the Roman statutes taken from Egypt. In response to this act of goodwill from the Kushites, the Romans moved their military frontier from Primis, maintaining a smaller guard post at Hiera Sykaminos, close to Syene.

Chapter - 10

The Legacy of Amanirenas

Amanirenas was the second of eight Kandakes who ruled the Kingdom of Kush. After her death around 10 BC, she was buried at the Jebel or Gebel Barkal royal cemetery, a sacred mountain in present-day Sudan. During her reign, she prevented the Roman Empire from conquering Kush and negotiated favorable treaty terms. Even after her death, the peace treaty between Kush and Rome remained in force. The trade partnership she created continued.

Kandake Amanirenas died knowing she had secured her kingdom's independence. To ensure that history accurately recorded her defeat of the Roman Empire, Kandake Amanirenas refused to return the bronze head of Caesar Augustus during negotiations for the peace treaty. This bronze piece, known as *The Meroë Head* or *Head of Augustus from Meroë*, was discovered around 1910 in modern Sudan. Its size is larger-than-life and clearly represents the features of Augustus. It is on display at the British Museum on Great Russell Street in London, U.K.

Glossary

AD	This is short for anno Domini, meaning in the year of our Lord. AD is the period after the birth of Jesus Christ, also known as CE or Common Era.
BC	This is short for before Christ, meaning the period before the birth of Jesus Christ. BC is also known as BCE or Before the Common Era.
Kingdom of Kush	Kush was an ancient kingdom in northeastern Africa, covering parts of modern Egypt and Sudan.
Kandake	Kandake was a term used for a member of the royal family, queen regent, or the mother of a king. It also referred to a queen who was a sole ruler. In Latin, it is written as *Candace*.
Nile River	The Nile River in northeastern Africa flows into the Mediterranean Sea.
Hieroglyphs	Hieroglyphs were a form of picture writing used by the Egyptians. It now describes picture writing by other ancient civilizations.

Stelae Stelae are ancient tablets made from stone used to record the names of important people like kings and queens and their activities.

Caesar Augustus Caesar Augustus was the first Roman Emperor. He was also known as Octavian or Gaius Octavius.

Nubia Nubia describes an area around the Nile River, beginning in southern Egypt around Aswan to the area where the Blue and White Nile Rivers meet.

The Meroë Head This is a large bronze representation of Caesar Augustus' head. It was taken from Roman Egypt during Kandake Amanirenas' battle with the Romans.

Emissaries People who are sent by a leader to go on a mission, usually to manage relationships between countries or nations.

Quiz

1. Who was Kandake Amanirenas?

    (a) Queen of Egypt
    (b) Queen Mother of Ethiopia
    (c) Queen of Kush
    (d) Queen Mother of Aksum

2. During what period did Kandake Amanirenas live?

    (a) AD
    (b) DE
    (c) JL
    (d) BC

3. Which empire threatened Kush's independence?

    (a) Roman
    (b) Ethiopian
    (c) Assyrian
    (d) Sudanese

4. Which leader did Amanirenas settle a peace treaty with?

    (a) Cleopatra
    (b) Caesar Augustus
    (c) Marc Anthony
    (d) Nero Claudius

Quiz Answers: **CDAB**

References

Ashby, Solange. "Priestess, Queen, Goddess: The Divine Feminine in the Kingdom of Kush." *The Routledge Companion to Black Women's Cultural Histories*, edited by Janell Hobson, Routledge, 2021, pp. 23-34. https://doi.org/10.4324/9780429243578.

Humphris, Jane and Thilo Rehren. "Iron production and the Kingdom of Kush: An Introduction to UCL Qatar's Research in Sudan." *Ein Forscherleben zwischen den Welten*, edited by Angelika Lohwasser and Pawel Wolf, Sonderheft MittSAG, 2014, pp. 177-190.

Smith, Stuart Tyson. "Revenge of the Kushites: Assimilation and Resistance in Egypt's New Kingdom Empire and Nubian Ascendancy over Egypt." *Empires and Diversity: On the Crossroads of Archaeology, Anthropology, and History*, edited by Gregory Areshian, Cotsen Institute of Archaeology Press, 2013, pp. 84-107.

Harkless, Necia Desiree. *Nubian Pharaohs and Meroitic Kings: The Kingdom of Kush*. Bloomington, Author House, 2006.

Adams, William Y. "The Kingdom and Civilization of Kush in Northeast Africa." *Nubia Corridor to Africa*, edited by William Y. Adams, Princeton University Press, pp. 775-789. http://www.ericlevy.com/Revel/Intro2/Kingdom%20and%20Civilization%20of%20Kush%20and%20North%20Africa.PDF.

Fun Fact About the Nile River

The Nile River, located in northeastern Africa, is the world's longest river. It is formed by three main rivers, the Blue Nile, Atbara or Black Nile, and the White Nile. It has an unusual flow pattern, moving from the south to the north into the Mediterranean Sea.

Other Books in the Heritage Collection

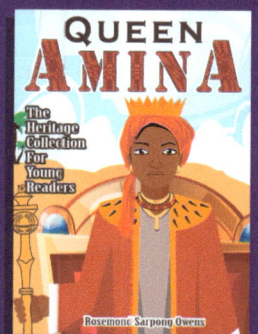
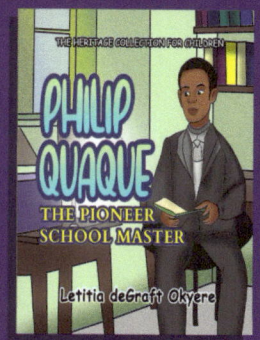

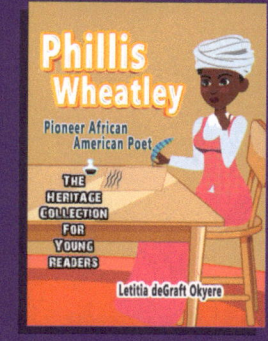
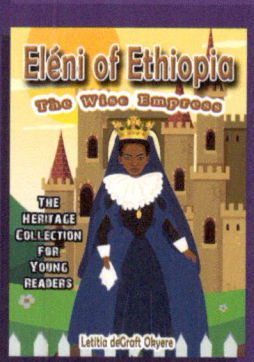
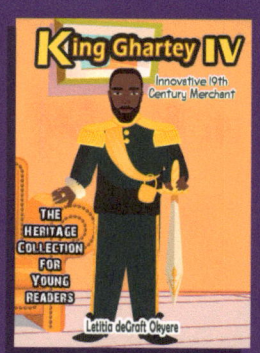
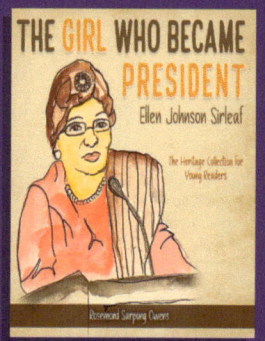
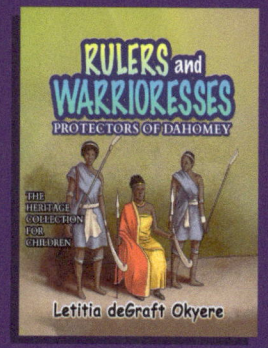
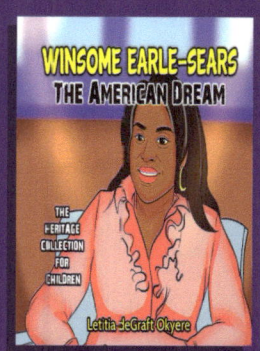
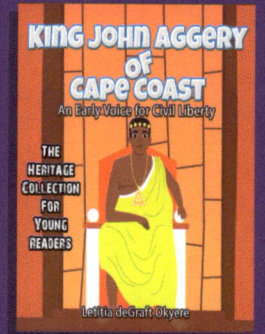

The End

www.ingramcontent.com/pod-product-compliance
Lightning Source LLC
Chambersburg PA
CBHW041405010526
44107CB00015B/1081